Trees

Coloring Book

Collection of Nature, Forests, Woods & Lonely Tree Landscapes, 44 Artist's Hand Drawings for Adults

Rachel Mintz

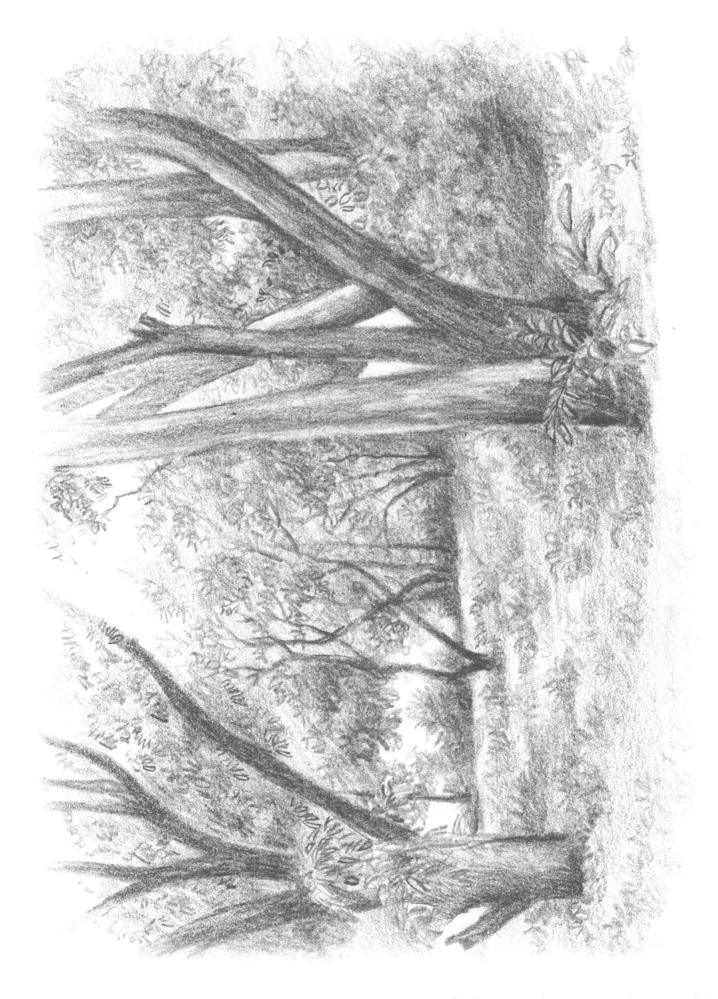

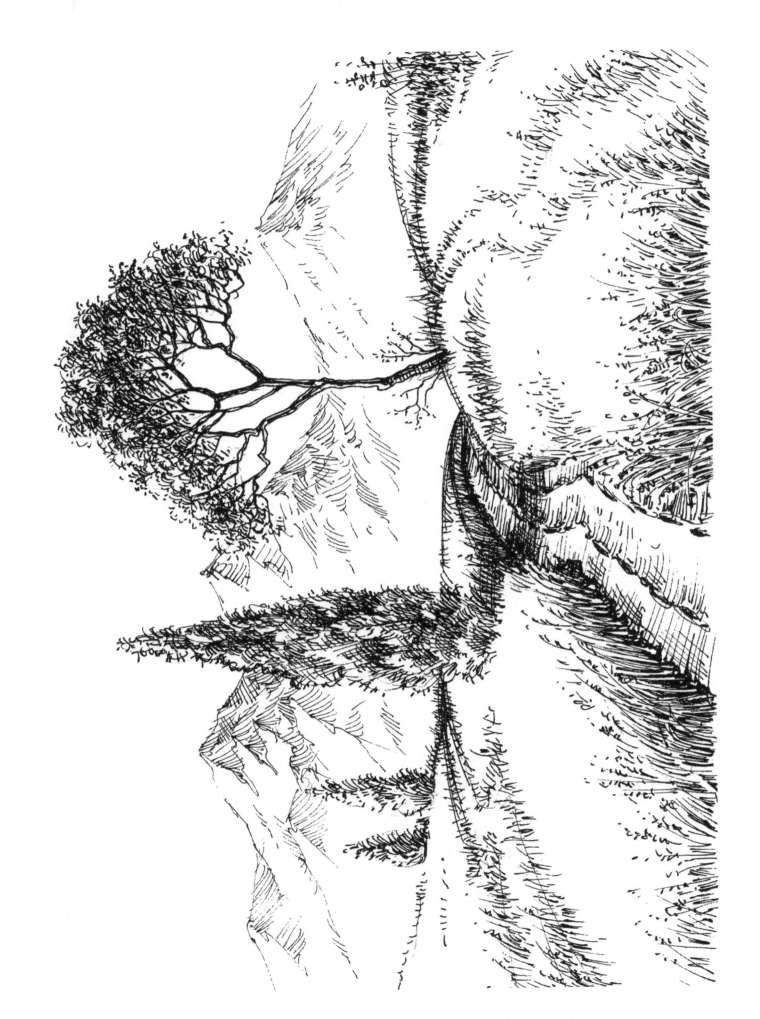

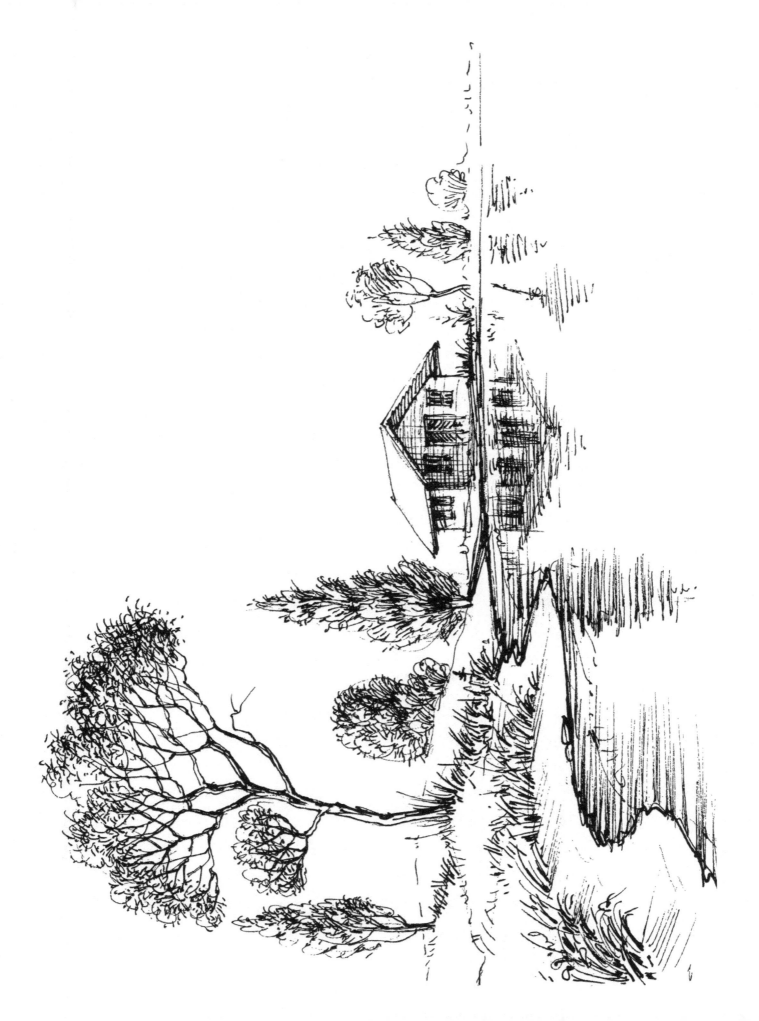

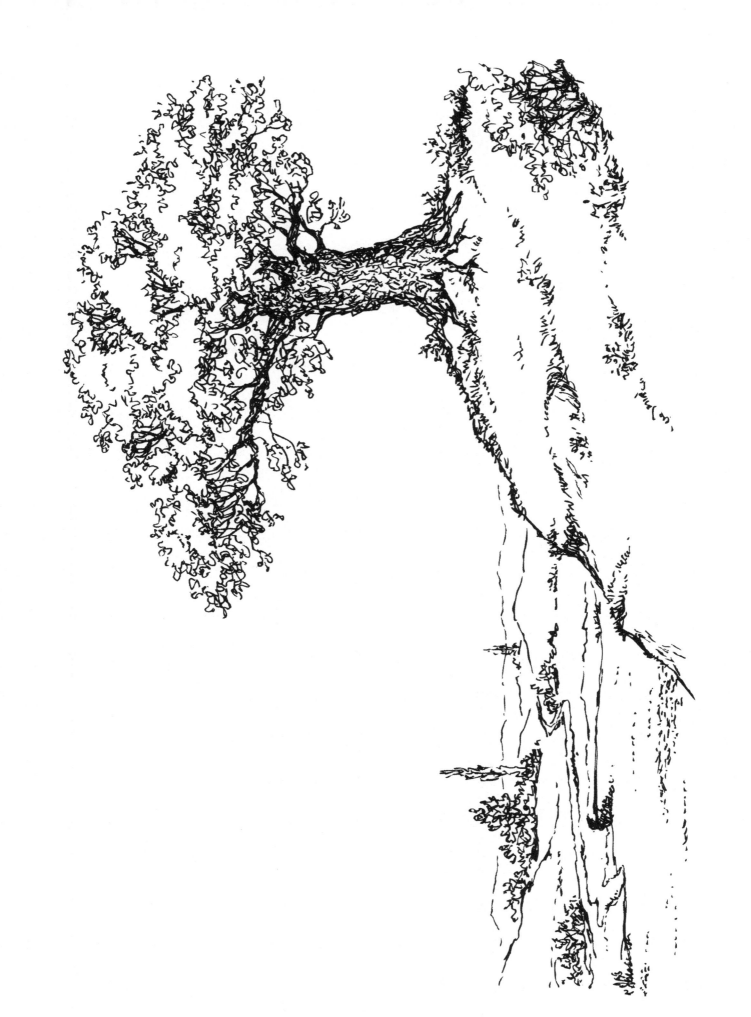

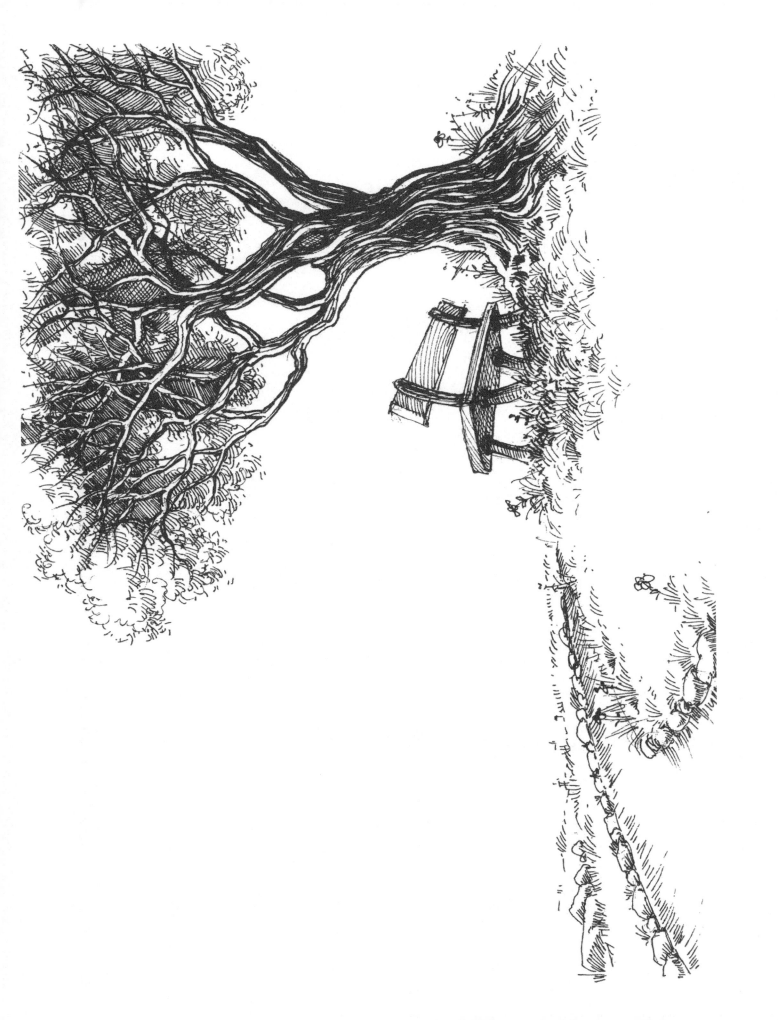

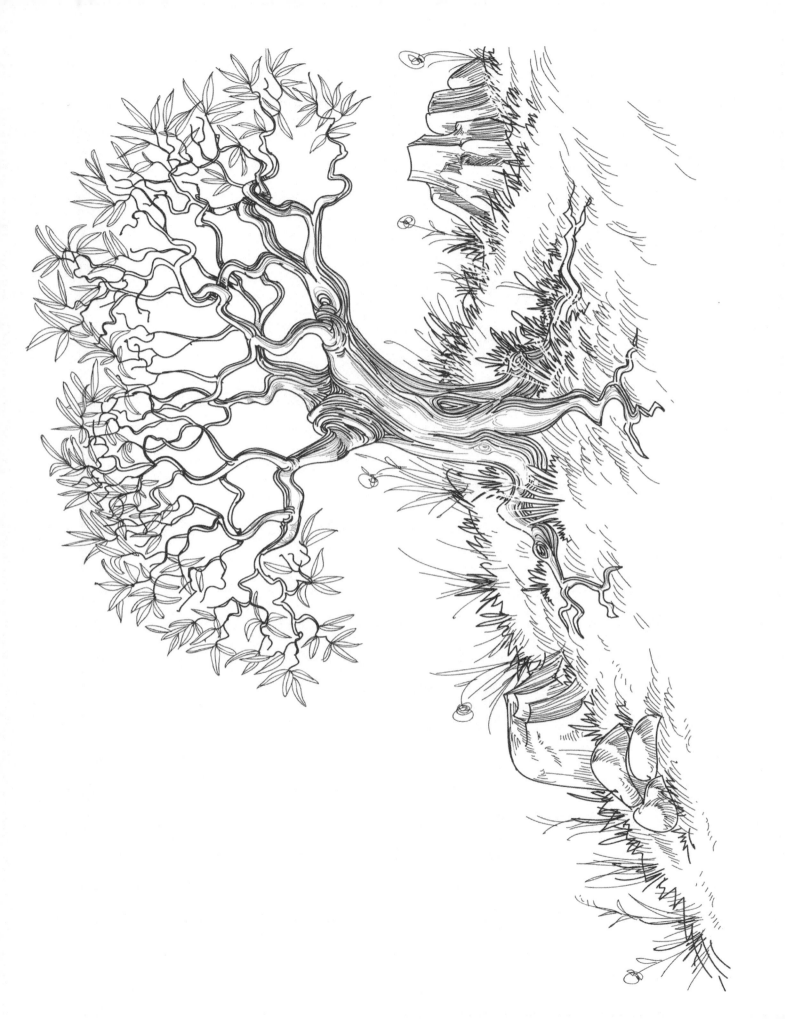

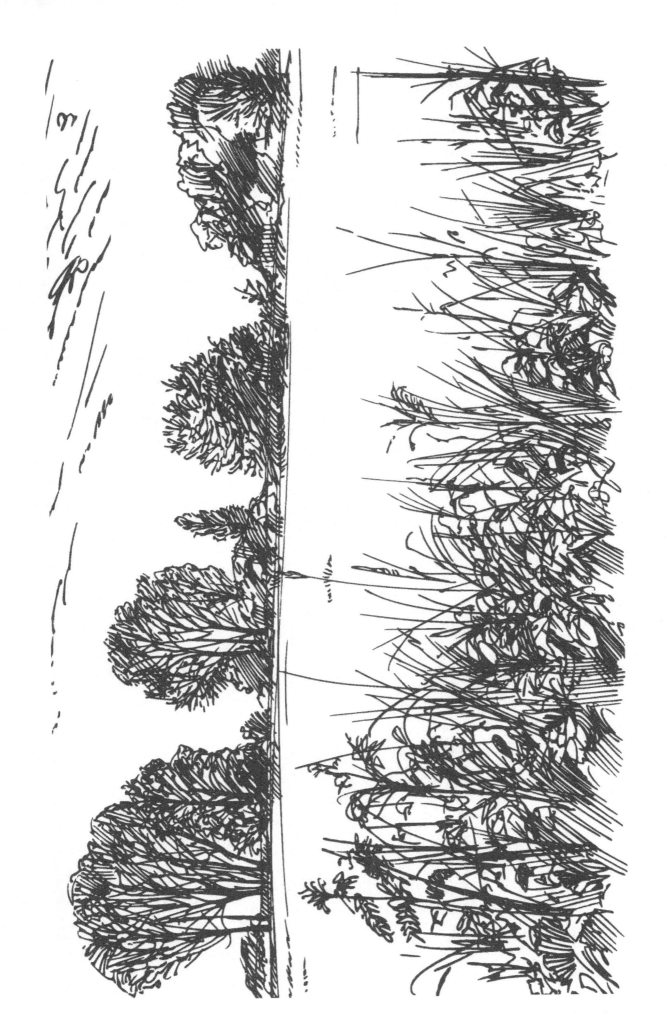

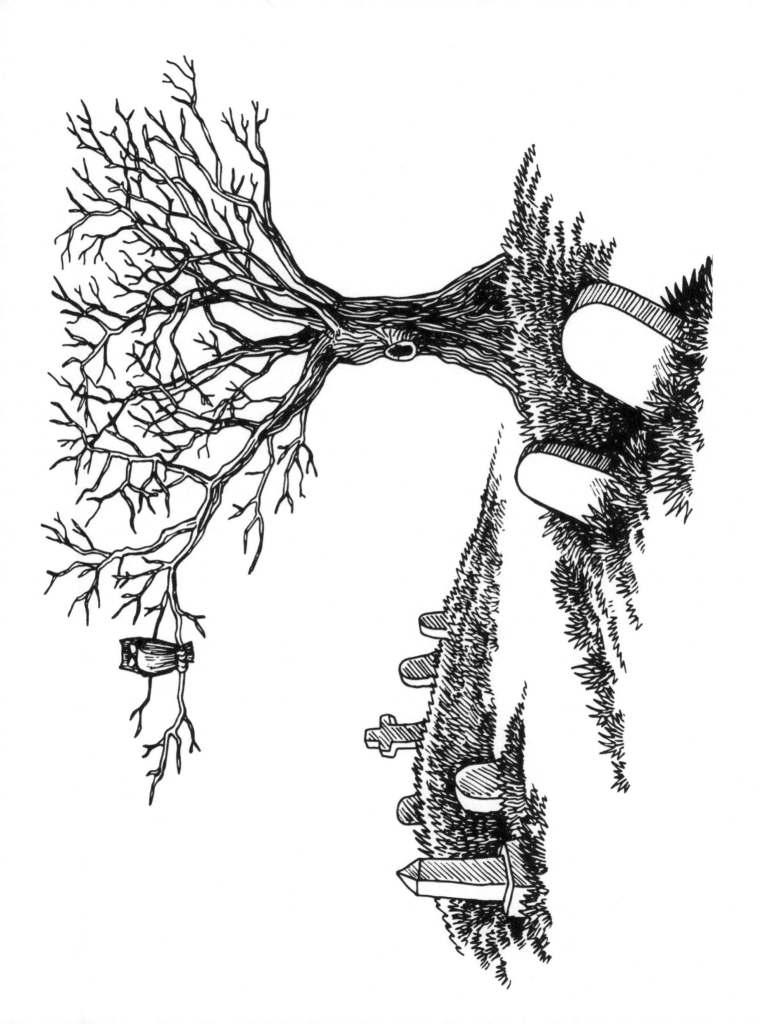

Thank you for coloring with us

More from our coloring books:

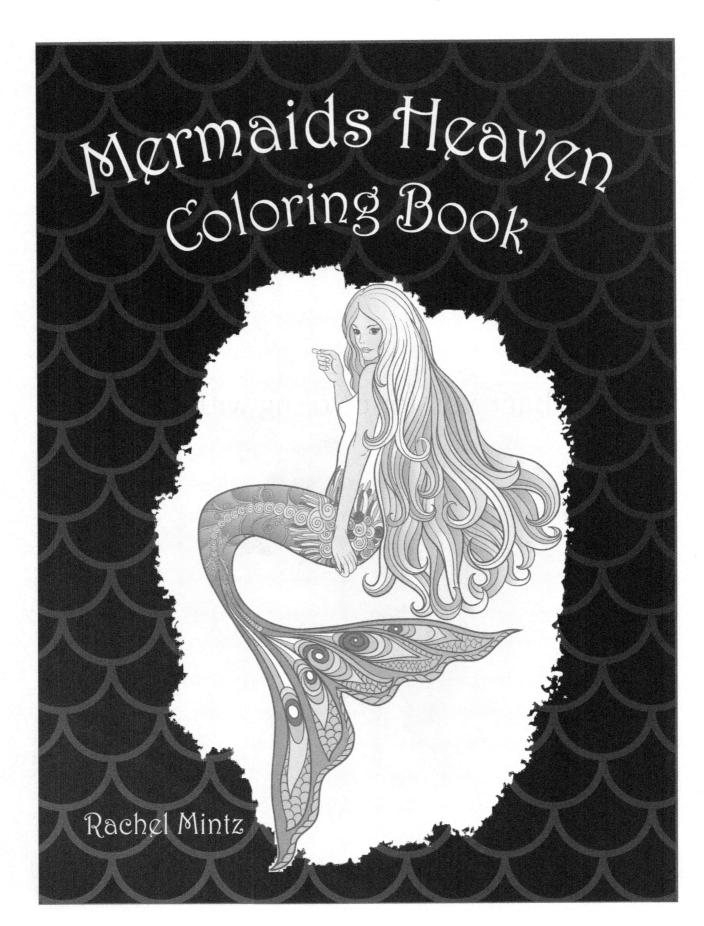

Mermaids Heaven
Coloring Book

Rachel Mintz

Seahorses
Coloring Book

Rachel Mintz

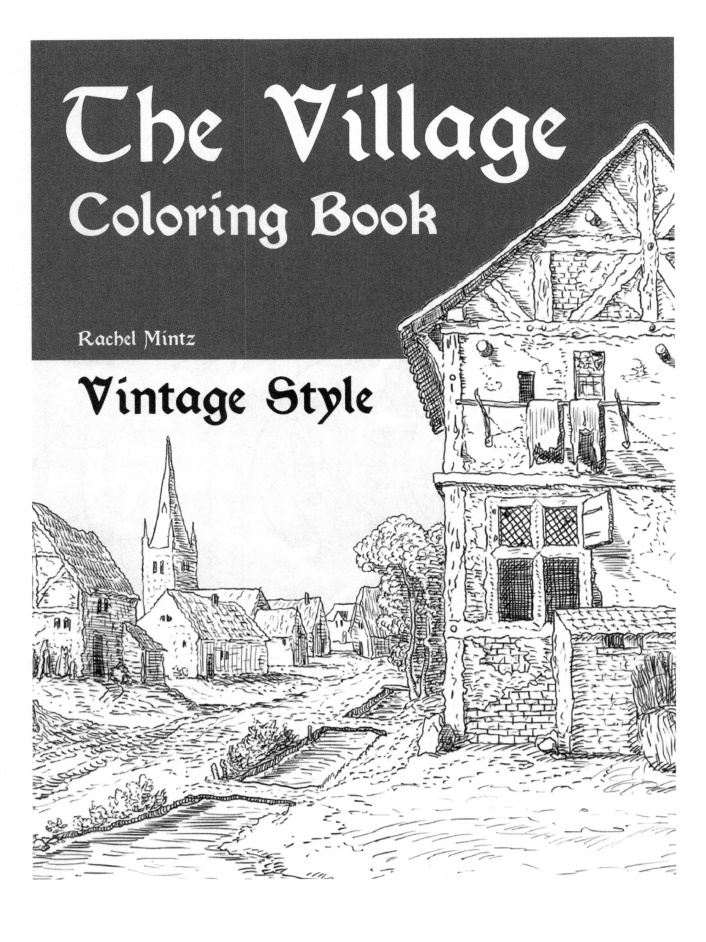

The Village
Coloring Book

Rachel Mintz

Vintage Style

Thank you for coloring with us

Made in United States
North Haven, CT
13 December 2022

28583972R00057